Memories

A collection of poems

From

Stuart McWilliam

Aka

Red Rose Man

<u>Young Love</u>

Explosive, spontaneous magical
attraction
Intense responsive interaction
The power of evolving love
Exciting like discovering treasure
trove

The beauty of your emerald eyes
Bringing delight and sheer surprise
Glowing brilliance of your golden
hair
Porcelain delicacy of skin so fair

Luscious lips of crimson red
Parted to display teeth, pearly white.
A picture of pure delight
Flashing in a gorgeous smile
Entranced was I by your class and
style

Scintillating sparking beautiful
appearance
Propelling my heart to find romance

Your whole being does me entrance
Totally captured, enraptured at first
glance

Two young lovers, united as one
Our love story has just begun
Fully committed without fears
Bonded together happily for years

TV dinner Date

Two lonely people, seeking romance
Cooking a meal, taking a chance
Sitting at a table, sharing a meal
Finding out how each other feel

Hoping the starter will tease
Whetting the taste buds, that will
please
Somethings can be taboo,
Like sharing an embarrassing tattoo

While serving the meal with some
charm
Oops! There goes the smoke alarm

Accept the wine he is now proffering
Better than the food – burnt offering

Time to serve up the sweet
Hoping it will be a treat
Will he enjoy the death by
chocolate?
Could he be your soul mate?

After doing all the cooking
Is this guy sweet, and good looking?
Will he have you in a trance?
Could this be a lasting romance?

Red Alert
(Printed Lennox Herald)

Nature strikes, snow, red warning
All clear tonight, snowed in this
morning
Snow so deep, temperature
dropping
Could this be caused by global
warming?

Everything grinding to a halt
Where are the gritters? Council at fault
Buses off, train not running also
Was it the wrong kind of snow?

The children are happy, not fools
This snow has closed all the schools
Drifting snow, high as a ten foot hedge
Children flying downhill on a sledge

No deliveries of milk or bread
Might as well stay in bed
Postal services also fail
One big plus – NO junk mail

Can't get to work causing economic burden
Not our fault says Nicola Sturgeon
Stand together be a good neighbour
Problem caused by the Tories and Labour

<u>Beautiful was she</u>
<u>(Printed Lennox Herald)</u>

She was beautiful,
Beautiful was she
And I loved her, oh I loved her
And I know that she loved me

She was beautiful
Beautiful was she
And it is her I'm longing to see
And know she longs to see me

She was beautiful
The apple of my eye
Then I lost her, I lost her
The day she did die

She still remains beautiful
Hear in my heart, my heart
I know we will be reunited
Never, never, more to be apart

Red Rose Day – Giving to the Living
(Printed Lennox Herald)

It is in giving that we receive
In giving we practice not to deceive
Like our condolence to people who
grieve
Earnestly attempting their sadness
to relieve

To the person confined to a
wheelchair
Who may feel invisible, un-noticed,
not there
Reach out your hand, show that you
care
As you give your time with them
share

Having recently lost my loving wife
I am experiencing loneliness in my
life
Now I'm learning to be giving
By handing out a rose to the living

The element of joy and surprise
Cab be seen shining in their eyes
With gratitude they will say
Thank you, you have made my day

Amazing how I and stranger draw
close
In the giving and receiving of a
single red rose
Often with hugs and beaming smiles
Will keep me going some extra miles

Red Nose day is well known
Where kindness and generosity is
shown
Let me here and now propose
A day of giving a single Red Rose

<u>Ode to HMRC</u>
<u>(Printed Lennox Herald)</u>

Now is the winter of my deepest
discontent
I write to HMRC my lament

Two certainties of life, taxes and
death
Doomed, doomed, we are all
doomed
With HMRC tax returns we are
consumed
Even after death they will have your
assets exhumed

I am eighty years old, in decline
Pile on the pain, HMRC demand for
late penalty fine
Did you hear my sharp intake of
breath?
Lesser of two evils, what do I
choose? My first option is death

In death surely I would find

Escape from HMRC – peace of mind
I am the man who gives out a single
red rose
Alas HMRC – not fit for purpose

I had a long and cherished dream
That I would escape the clutches of
this machine
My dream became a dreadful
nightmare
I am plagued by telephone robotic
voices – they don't care

The government say from torture
practices they will refrain
Yet they are driving me insane
You think all is well, all is fine
Have you tried to get HMRC online?

All of your life you work and slave
Final release from HMRC – final
release in your grave
Now you are remembered as Stuart
the Late
HMRC will backdate your taxes and
take them from your estate

My final attempt to laugh and joke
HMRC for my taxes owed
Payment cheque is in the pocket of
my shroud
I am being cremated, the cheque
and I will disappear
Both gone in a puff of smoke.

<u>A Special Relationship
(Printed Lennox Herald)</u>

When two kindred spirits share
Their individual ability to care
Where compromise is made
Sharing in sunshine and shade

Together through life's highs and
lows
Fused as one, their love grows
Sharing triumphs conquering woes
Enraptured by the fragrance of a
rose

Building bridges when needs
must
Learning each other to truly trust
Finding out new things to do
Remembering to say, Darling I love
you

Time has passed, years gone by
My darling, my love, you did die
Ten years of dementia
Was our long goodbye

Heartache and tears I try to hide
Deep within me you reside
My eternal hope
With you to abide

Reflection
(Printed Lennox Herald)

At this time of life
What am I seeing?
What is going on within?
The depth of my being

I've loved, I've laughed, I've cried
I've mourned your passing when you
died
I will not fall or be despaired
I'm holding on to the love we shared

What about the here and now
What lonely furrow will I now
plough?
Will I rise like the eagle and soar
Embraced by our love for evermore

Now I must overcome the gloom
Knowing when you passed through
death's door
You've only moved to another room
And we will be reunited for evermore

Dream Traveller

From a mountain top high
I can visualise with my mind's eye
Crossing borders and frontiers
Silently peacefully without fears

Travelling the world in my dreams
Crossing oceans, fording streams
In my memory store I find
Journeys I can take in my mind

Now I pause, my darling, thinking of
you
And the love we shared, so faithful
and true
Remembering things we did, we
said
I recapture in my head

If we could live our life again
I would start with that night when
I escorted you home, kissed at the
garden gate

Asked you for a date, you became
my soul mate

<u>Love – Emotion of the Heart</u>

Love, emotion of the heart
Two enjoined till death us part
Both hearts beating in harmony
Becoming one, you and me

The excitement of that first date
I was early, you were late
I was content, happy to wait
For you my love, my darling soul
mate

Our time together has flown so fast
Remembering yu – living in the past
Sharing together each living breath
Sadly we are parted by your death

Alas, I alone remain
O to live our life again
To walk with you hand in hand
Eternally in the Promised Land

Feelings Declared

Today the sun is shining
The sky is blue
Bringing back my memories of you
Times spent together – now apart
Darling you still fill my heart

There is a light summer breeze
Rustling the leaves on the trees
It is like hearing your voice
Causing my heart to rejoice

The scenery down by the shore
Opens up another door
Darling it is you that I adore
Oh – To hold you in my arms once
more

As the tides ebb and flow
This I want you to know
Since you passed on from this life

Thanks for being a wonderful wife!

I Remember You

I remember you, in hot summer days
How your hair shone in the sun's
rays
Your hair was blond, your eyes so
green
The most beautiful girl I've ever
seen

Walking together in the fields,
beside streams,
You were the girl of my dreams
Your lovely smile, beautiful face
To hold you tight in an embrace

Pausing now and then to kiss
Life with you was pure bliss
I'm picturing you in my mind's eye
I miss you darling, why did you die

You were so warm, full of life

Brightened every day when you
became my wife
Looking back, I'm happy we met
Living today with no regret

Smile of my Life

One of your smiles, to me happiness
brings
I rejoice, my heart sings
I feel your presence, your fragrance
clings
Memories of you, love eternal
springs

Once upon a time you entered my
life
My dreams were answered, you
became my wife
The joy of living, so sweet
You were my darling, I felt complete

How can I explain this deep
emotion?
Two young lovers in deep devotion
We mem not really by chance

Bound together in rapturous romance

My darling, my love, so beautiful and
fair
You were so gentle, so kind, and full
of care
In this life we climbed to heights so
high
Till that final day you did die

Now on earth I still remain
Youi have risen to a higher plane
I mourn the loss, feel the pain
Yet I still rejoice in your eternal gain

When my time comes to die
Hopefully to your side I'll fly
To live eternally side by side
Together forever to abide

Unspoken Words
(Printed Lennox Herald)

The silence of words not heard
No expression that you cared
The feelings of desertion
Through the lack of conversation

Then if only, what might have been
The gradual loss of love's dream
Nail your colours to the mast
Treat every day like it was your last

Remember the feelings when you
first met
Keep them going, live without regret
Make every effort, to have effect
Treat each other with great respect

Love shared is about give and take
Keep your vows, all others forsake
To each other be true and steadfast
Then your relationship will surely
last

Your journey through life, no matter
how long
Remember it is to each other you
belong
When that day arrives that breaks
your heart
The final parting, till death us did
part

Then comes the times of
remembrance
The lasting memories of great
romance
Recalling your beautiful wife
Having shared such a wonderful life

<u>Your Smile</u>

One of your smiles to me happiness
brings
I rejoice, my heart sings
I feel your presence, your fragrance
clings
Memories of you, love eternal
springs

Once upon a time you entered my
life
My dreams were answered, you
became my wife
The joy of living was so sweet
You were my darling, I felt complete

How can I explain this deep
emotion?
Two young lovers in true devotion
We met not really by chance
Bound together in rapturous
romance

My darling, my love, beautiful and
fair

You were so gentle so kind, fill of care
In this life we climbed heights so high
Until that final day you did die

Today

Today be thankful for the air we breathe
Be thankful for the freedom to believe
To practice to love and not deceive
Life is better when we give, we also receive

In your life show love and care
Make a difference, bring happiness not despair
Avoid a frown, show a smile
Be willing to walk that extra mile

Be kind to the stranger in need
Overcome anger, malice and greed
Give to the poor, the hungry feed

Do it now, don't delay, act with speed

Then this world a better place will be
When we make the effort, changes you will see
Together we can do this, you and me
Spreading love and joy, living in harmony

Today, now is the starting place
Meeting people, face to face
Bringing love lasting peace to the human race
Filling lives of others with dignity and grace

Valley of tears

Locked in your valley of tears
Confronted by your inner fears
Lost in a lonely place
Escaping the world you cannot face

Lost in darkness and despair
Feeling alone, does anyone care?
Struggling to make an impression
Locked in the pit of depression

Life seems like one long grind
When troubled thoughts cloud your
mind
Wil you ever feel release
Will this torment ever cease?

Yes, you can overcome
Escape from darkness into the sun
It was a hard road, not much fun
But now, finally you have won

It's been a while

It's been a while
Since I last saw you smile
Time has not healed my aching
heart
Since you left, now we are apart

Now I'm in a lonely place
Miss you darling, and your lovely
face
It's been a while since we parted
Leaving me sad and broken hearted

Now I feel so alone
Lost without you, since you've been
gone
It's been a while since our last kiss
Darling it's you I miss

Like driftwood on a lonely beach
We are out of town, out of reach
As the tides ebb and flow
Darling why did you have to go?

<u>September Song</u>

In my life it is September
Reliving the past, my love, you I
remember
You filled my life in so many ways
Sweet memories, happy days

My darling who was I to you
What did you see in me?
That night you came in to my life
Did you plan to be my wife?

Did I meet your expectation?
Did I fill you with elation?
Did I make your life worthwhile?
You brightened mine with your
lovely smile

Life's journey of fifty seven years
Brought love and joy, and a few
tears
My darling, my love so tender
Sweet thoughts of you I remember
Now in my life, in September

Twilight Years

How many roads have you travelled
on?
How many days have come and
gone
Since your life began, when you
were born
Now twilight years, surviving life's
storm

Each day of life, memories
accumulated
Our past, our present, formulated
Living then just for each day
Never thinking of being old and grey

Now we recall memories of old
When we were young, strong and
bold
Never thinking we would age
Until now in our dotage

Thankful for a wonderful life

The love of a darling wife
For family and friends
Till life's final journey ends

Thresholds of Life
(Printed Lennox Herald)

Doors that open,
Doors that close
Doors of opportunity and chance
Doors of a blossoming romance

Going to school to learn
Starting work, to earn
Getting a trade apprenticeship
Part of a team, building a ship

National Service in the Army
Gun Fitter craftsman in the REME
Basic training trade and military
Posted abroad to Germany

Returning home apprenticeship
complete
A beautiful girl I then did meet

She was the love of my life
Engaged, married, she became my
wife

<u>Simply Read</u>
<u>(Printed Lennox Herald)</u>

This is a story simply read
Of the memories stored in my head
It tells of love, its chemistry
Affair of the heart, life's mystery

Love an enigma about emotion
Where two entwined together in
devotion
Two hearts and minds embraced in
adoration
Like the effect of a magical mystical
potion

How can I explain the feelings?
That send the heart and senses
reeling
When two lovers find each other
appealing

Declaring their love, to all revealing

What is this strange thing called love
With mere words how can I prove?
It is an adventure worth exploring
For I know, its lasting and enduring

There is a beginning without end
Enjoy all the precious moments you
spend
Together two combined as one
You will understand when your love
has begun

Depression (then)

Depression, a place or dark despair
It's not uncommon, nor is it rare
It's a place you don't want to be
When you're surrounded by
darkness
And you cannot escape, you cannot
see

It is not being physically blind

It is a darkness of the mind
It is a place for fear and dread
Residing deep within your head

Some people say "Give yourself a shake"
Not realising inside you quake
And find it difficult decisions to make
Caught in a trap like an addiction you can't break

On the outside you look healthy and well
Inside your head is a living hell
Inside that awful feeling of dread
Think you would be – better off dead

Nervous and anxious feeling so low
Which way to turn, where can you go
Fight or flight, words often said
But they do not know what's going on in my head

In this mental battle you feel alone

Longing to be normal to overcome strife
I am a human being, not made of stone
Struggling to cope on my journey through life

Depression (Now)

The darkness is lifted, now there is light
With kind understanding and medical attention
Aided by the right medication
I'm happy, I'm cheerful, full or elation

Gone is that feeling of low self esteem
No longer a nightmare, now I have a dream
Gone is the feeling of being second best
I know who I am now, my mind is at rest

Instead of that battle with others to compare
I've learned to give of myself and to share
It is in giving we also receive
That's how I feel now, it's what I believe

At last I'm off the treadmill
Life more settled and tranquil
I'm past middle age, but not over the hill
Life is still an adventure, to follow and fulfil

I have learned from the past
As backward my mind I cast
Time does not stand still, nothing really lasts
The present, today is what I've got
I am happy and content with my lot
Take it, grasp it, we only get one shot.

Magnetic Attraction

Drawn like a moth to the light
My Darling, it was love at first sight
Like the recurring sound of a sweet
refrain
I'm longing to see you once again

Love an overwhelming emotion
Filled with awe and adoration
To me so real I had no doubt
Like refreshing rain after drought

You increased the beat of my heart
Miss you so much now we are apart
That joyful feeling when you appear
You were a vision of beauty, my
dear

In my heart, memories I hold
You were worth more than gold
Thankfully together we grew old
In eternity our future will unfold

Disaster of Divorce (an observation)

Dissolving of what once was
What was the reason, what was the cause?
What happened – to you and me?
Lost – our first love, failure to agree

Married life started out so well
You and I together we did gel
Then children came along
Happy family, what went wrong/

Married life needs give and take
True to each other, all others forsake
Problems arise through selfishness
Bliss dissolves into a hellish mess

Often our life can be dramatic
Divorce can be so traumatic
What happened to love's young dream?
Gone is the joy, you want to scream

Time elapses, what happens now?
Seems so long ago you shared that
vow
Time to get on with life, pick up the
threads
To rebuild a life shattered in shreds

An extra marital affair
Bringing heartache and despair
Trust and hope beyond repair
Suspicions aroused, trace of lipstick,
a hair

No man or woman is an island
Joined together by a gold band
Promises to love and obey
If only actions would match what we
say

As the marriage came to a halt
Haunting questions, was it my fault
The pain of your spouse's
indiscretion
That despairing feeling of rejection

What of the children feeling bereft
When you split up, one parent left
Love them pray for them each day
Lift that dark cloud of grey
Turn it in to bright blue
That one day they may find love too
Get married and say "I Do"

Terrestrial Bliss

Feet firmly planted on the ground
True bliss with you I found
Sharing a loving devotion
Together locked in emotion

Walking and talking on our way
Close relationship day by day
Pausing now and then to embrace
We discovered our loving place

Travelling life's journey you and me
Fulfilling what was meant to be
Your beauty and your beguiling
smile
You always went the extra mile

Alas our journey came to an end
When you died, my darling, lover,
friend
Still I feel your closeness yet
My darling love, you I can't forget

Till we meet once again
Here in my heart you will remain
Bound together by a love so strong
My darling to you I belong

Magic Moments

The moment two people meet
A shot in the dark
Love's initial spark
The when and the where
The how and the why
Without prior arrangement
You meet someone who
Will have a profound effect
On you and your future
Life as the song goes
Fools give you reasons
Wise men never try
But that one enchanted

Evening can arrive
Out of the blue
You meet that someone
Who totally captures your heart?
That your life
Can never be complete
Without them
This I know
This I see
Yes
It happened to me

Risk Street Mystery
(Printed Lennox Herald)

It was the day of snow so deep
It caused our Brian to weep
Ominous was the location – Risk
Street
Now I will tell you what made Brian
Greet

Gingerly making his way home
Clutching his precious 'carry oot'
Conditions dicey underfoot

He stopped to dig a car oot

Brian laid his carry oot on the
ground
Finally clearing away snow
His carry oot could not be found
It was now buried under the snow

Light damage to the car's rear
reflector
Brian considered getting a metal
detector
To uncover his precious cargo
Lost without trace beneath the snow

Brian was with shock and horror
filled
Very unhappy, definitely not thrilled
Was the contents of his carry oot
brewed or distilled?
On a happier not – at least it will be
well chilled

Childhood Lost

How does a Syrian child cope?
Seven year's old, life without hope
He must wonder what life is for
He knows nothing but bombing
carnage and war

This world created as a wonderful
place
For the benefit of the human race
How far have we fallen, our actions
a disgrace?
Our behaviour has reached its
lowest base

How we long for peace not hate?
How long will we have to wait?
To rid the world of murder malice
and greed
To turn weapons into ploughshares,
cultivate and feed

Up till now there is no respite
As warring factions continue to fight
Each side claiming they are right

But all contributing to the childrens'
plight

Loving You

Loving you is what I do
My life spent adoring you
Without you darling, I'm so alone
My heart is empty since you've been
gone

Our love – like a tender plant grew
Flourishing through seasons, me
and you
The merging and melting of our
beings
To our dwelling place where love
reigns

Floating on a summer breeze
Whispering love amidst the trees
Walking hand in hand by gentle
streams
Fulfilling each other's dreams

Flying high on gossamer wings

Two hearts in time, romantic music
sings
Our love united in exchanging rings
My darling the loving memory to me
clings

Final Journey

Your final journey
To be buried in the ground
Mourners are attending
But Vale of Leven Cemetery cannot
be found

Surely you would like to know
That the mourners can find the way
to go
Arriving in the Vale, easy to get lost
For the cemetery, there are no
signposts

Even locals giving directions are
unsure
You could end up on Carman Moor
So WDC please help our vexation
By displaying signpost in cemetery
direction

Make the final journey easy to
navigate
So we can arrive on time, not be late
Help us to pay our last respect
Signpost for the cemetery, please
erect.

Childhood Robbery

Syrian refugee children far from
home
Living in camps in Lebanon
Suffering in Syria under despotic
rule
Robbed of childhood, cannot go to
school

Menial work is now their lot
Normal childhood they have not

Struggling to manage, trying to cope
Life is so empty, devoid of hope

Yet even now they express
A desire to progress
That one day could be reconciled
Return and Syria rebuild

Childhood robbery it is so wrong
Lost children have nowhere to
belong
Till adults of this world unite
To end forever the childrens plight.

Marion (Afterwards)

Marion, it's been a year since you
died
I am still crying inside
My memories of you are so sweet
How I long once again we will meet

Each day as I walk down the street
I wish my beautiful wife to meet
Each step I take I walk with you

Remember our love so good and so true

I picture you in every scene
From your childhood into a teen
And as a woman – I still dream
You filled my heart with love supreme

I have to write, to let you know
I can never let you go
Yes, I know that you have gone
That is why I feel so alone

I wander to places we have been
Recapturing our young lovers dream
The thrilling joy of our romance
How you smiled and loved to dance

Thank you for our long goodbye
Realising that you did die
You are gone to a better place
I long to see you again – face to face

Early Morning Story

Beneath the canopy of dark lowering
cloud
Bright shining light of early morn
Silver blue streaked with wisps of
white
Another day is born

Trees adorned in autumnal glory
Another chapter in life's story
Leaves of amber and of gold
Nature's beauty does unfold

Man with limited power and might
Could not create such a sight
Look around this earthly realm
Surely God is at the helm

The seasons come and go
Times to plant, times to sow
Times to nurture, times to grow
Times to harvest, times to mow

Our earthly sojourn in bound by time

Sometimes in life, mountains to climb
Then find peaceful valleys to recline
Enjoy the wonders of God's design

Seasons of our lives, anticipation of spring
The warmth of sunshine summer does bring
In autumn, slowing down, leaves turning brown
Winter's cold and snow comes down

Summertime?

I remember one fortnight in May
Wall to wall sunshine every day
This I found hard to believe
As this weather flattered to deceive

Why should I show surprise?
The norm is continual grey skies
Summer days when cold winds did blow
Followed by rain, hail and snow

In our town which built the 'Cutty Sark'
Maybe it should have been Noah's Ark
How often has the river been in flood?
Leaving shop floors covered in mud

Weather forecasters, Dumb and Dumber
Always promised a barbecue summer
Sadly with lasting regret
We don't enjoy barbecues in the wet

We should not find all of this strange
Green people tell us – Climate Change
My question of the wise and sage
How did we emerge from the Ice Age?

Is it just money making schemes
Can man control the Gulf and Jet Streams?
No my name is not Michael

I believe weather, climate move in a cycle.

<u>Alone</u>

Now that you my love have gone
I feel empty and so alone
Together we would often laugh
Then I was whole, now I'm half

Death it can be so cruel
How we lived to the full
Being near you brought so much joy
You were my girl, I was your boy

When I met you I was over the moon
Two young lovers, fully in tune
We were so happy in simple ways
You filled my life with wonderful days

Today I miss you so much
Your loving smile, your warm touch
Still inside I ache with pain
O my love to hold you once again

It was with great joy and pride
I was filled when you became my
bride
My darling wife of fifty seven years
Help me overcome my sadness and
tears

Marion, my darling it is you I adore
To have to hold to love for evermore
To meet again joined in serenity
Bound together for eternity

Echoes

Echoes of our times gone by
So in love, you and I
Miss you, since our long goodbye
Even now inside I cry

My darling you were so unique
Without you, life is so bleak
Lost you, when you fell ill
My empty heart, only you can fill

I see you now, vision of radiance

Our lives so full or romance
I loved you from my first glance
O to embrace you as we dance

Even now as I walk the street
Wishing that you I'd meet
I know that this cannot be
Until we are united in eternity

Grateful Life

Be grateful for the life you live
Do not take, learn to give
Forsake malice and greed
Share love, care for those in need

King Solomon asked for wisdom
Not for wealth and power
All his splendour could not compare
To the beauty of a lily flower

Let us every day to learn
To show to others our concern
A word, a gesture, in time of need
Sow some love, plant a seed

Our time on earth is not too long
Let us do right, avoid the wrong
Let others know that they belong
Spread joy and happiness with a
song

Marion (Later on)

Thoughts of you, images in my head
Alive to me, although you are dead
Recalling our love, words we said
I'm so thankful that we wed

In my mind it's you I'm seeing
How you thrilled my inner being
I was both stirred and shaken
My love for you did awaken

Darling you had beautiful eyes
My life you filled with surprise
How we loved to dance and sing
The sweet memories, I still cling

My life with you was never dull
Each day was different, always full

I miss you my darling very much
Your dazzling smile, your kiss, your
loving touch

I close my eyes and see you here
Longing to hold you, feel you near
I know for now this cannot be
Longing to be with you throughout
eternity

Each passing day, I cling on
To be with you, where you have
gone
Life is good, yet bittersweet
Haste the day till again we meet

With you my love always joy not
gloom
You were my bride, I was your
groom
We made this vow till death us do
part
My love you died, but still remain in
my heart

Ode to Snowflakes

Who are you that seeks to decry
The remembrance to shoes for
peace did die
From your comfortable modern life
You fail to honour the dead of strife

You are ignorant of their story
They died for peace, not seeking
glory
That we may be free, you and I
That is the reason they did die

In that freedom you have a voice
In your life you have a choice
Their life for ours was the price
Of their supreme sacrifice

None of us seek to glorify war
They thought peace worth dying for
Honour them and their martyrdom
Bringing to you peace and freedom

Memories of Marion

Marion I remember a day
We did not meet
I saw you from across the street
You wore a royal blue mohair coat
Tight fitting at the waist, you looked
so neat

When at last we did meet
You were in my house
My heart then skipped a beat
My head was spinning in a whirl
I was in love with a most beautiful
girl

Your hair so blonde, your eyes so
green
The most beautiful girl I'd ever seen
Head over heels, my heart went
overboard
Totally captivated, you alone I
adored

Our courtship was a wondrous thing
That I rejoice in remembering

You filled my life with so much joy
You were my girl, I was your boy

Our wedding arrange I am sure in
heaven
To last for years, all fifty seven
We were so close my dear
sweetheart
And the vow we made, till death us
do part

In the midst of life
Death came as a thief
We shall be reunited
That is my steadfast belief

<u>Marion</u>

On December Twenty Fifteen
I lost Marion, my lovely Queen
Ending a wonderful life my dream
Darling in my life you reigned
supreme

Our journey through life
Was exciting, electrifying
Marred only by your dying
I remember your love and passion
My beautiful delightful Marion

When first we met
Drawn together like a strong magnet
Precious enough memories linger on
No ifs, no buts, no regrets

Full and filled to overflowing
Our love for each other growing
Blossoming like a flower divine
Thank my darling for being mine

Marion I thank for our long goodbye

Softening the blow and loss when
you did die
Better to have loved and lost
Than never to have loved at all

Marion now that you are gone
I am left here all alone
You leave the fragrance of a rose
Just after a springtime rain
Cherished memories still remain

<u>Marion You know I love to sing</u>

Marion You know I love to sing
In knowing you I became a king
I felt I was seated on a throne
But now you're gone I'm so alone

The future is dim and drear
All because you are not here
My thoughts are now locked in the
past
As my mind is backward cast
Happiness will return one sweet day

When I hear you say
Reunited at last

Marion I often say your name
Trying to relive our love again
I long to recapture your lovely smile
Your sweet face that did me beguile

Every life has a beginning
And an end
From the very start
You stole my heart
I never wanted us to part
But in death you fell asleep
I cry alone as tears I weep

Help me Lord to know your will
That Marion has a place in heaven
to fill
She will hear your loving words of
encouragement
Well done my good and faithful
servant

May Day Call

It was in the early morning
In the month of May
My phone rang, start of a new day
I hear a voice, sweet dulcet tones
The lady is called Flavia Jones

She is of Welsh and Indian descent
Presently single, without a gent
Romance for her now must wait
As she cares for her mother of
ninety eight

Flavia's accent did me perplex
This is a girl from Sussex
Her voice sounds sweet and
moderate
I can't believe she is forty eight

I am Stuart, the guy Flavia has
called
Thinning white hair, not yet bad

She said my voice sounded young,
full of fun
Was surprised to hear I am eighty
one

Flavia thank you for brightening my
day
Lifting my spirits in a happy way
Your hair is dark, your eyes are grey
Perhaps in another life
We could be man and wife

That's Life
(Printed Lennox Herald)

Are you a winner or a loser?
Are you quite sober or are you a
boozer
Are you a giver or a taker?
Are you a potential heartbreaker?

In love we all take a chance
In finding the right person for
romance

Do you feel safe flirting with a
stranger?
Or have a feeling you may be in
danger

In your life are you feeling insecure?
Of many things are you unsure
Deep inside you're longing to meet
The guy, the girl to sweep you off
your feet

You have just had your first date
The next day you can hardly wait
Mulling over how, where, when
You can get together once again

Moving on, now reaching stage two
Mutual love and admiration
Exchanging the words, I Love You,
Embracing, kissing, feelings of
adoration

Now realise in your heart
You can't live your lives apart
Now you and me
Decide to become we

Flying High

Flying high, wind in my hair
Feeling your love, knowing you care
Rising above the daily grind
All I need, in you I find

Floating on air, in blue skies above
Captivated completely by your love
Girl of my dreams, love of my heart
Be mine forever, never to part

Let's walk together every day
Being happy all the way
Looking forward to reach our goal
Glad to be working, not on the dole

Enjoying all the time we spend
Loving forever, right to the end
Thankful for a wonderful life
The blessings of being man and wife

<u>Eyes</u>

It has been said, that beauty is in the eye of the beholder, a true observation.
It has also been said that the eyes are the windows of the soul – also true.
Of all the facial features, the eyes are the most expressive.
We can even smile with our eyes.
We can look appealingly, we can look lovingly, adoringly and seductively.
We can also look angrily, menacingly.
We can look pensively, thoughtfully, caringly.
That look that says I love you, I want to be with you always.
Eyes that can gaze steadily into yours, no sign of avoidance.
The eyes that show recognition, that show appreciation, thankfulness.
We talk about face to face confrontation.

Eye to eye contact expressing pure delight, a reflection between two lovers of their loving relationship. Eyes that shine with happiness and joy. Even the slight shy glance can register that feeling of attraction, mutual affection, leading us to full romantic bliss, with that first embrace, that first kiss, with eyes shut or open.
Darling my eyes are blue, yours are green, and you are the most beautiful woman I have ever seen
With you I am king, and you are my queen

What If

What if on that night we met
I had returned home late
And you had already left my home
Would we our separate ways have gone?

Thankfully I arrived in time
To escort you home, it was sublime

We talked we kissed at your back
door
I asked you for a date, you said yes
I was thrilled to the core

Our Date
I was early, you were late
My heart was beating at a faster rate
A bit frustrated, in a tizzy
Fearing I might get a dizzy

You arrived and quelled my fear
Thank you for turning up my dear
From that day on our love just grew
Now we're as one, me and you

October Odyssey
(Printed Lennox Herald)

Started with early morning chill
Fresh air for your lungs to fill
Midday the sky is blue
This month we had the jab for flu

From my window a panoramic view

Dumbarton Castle, split in tow
Further afield, the Crags, Dumbuck Hill
A wondrous scene my eyes do fill

Strolling over old Dumbarton Bridge
Looking over the parapet ridge
Tide is high, not a ripple seen
Calming, feeling so serene

Out and about, meeting people
At the end of the street, church with steeple
The brightness of this autumnal day
Lifts the spirit, brightens my way

Dumbarton, town of wide pavement
But narrow of street
Traffic jams drivers lament
Fosters road rage, make you greet

Modern age of computer and Wi-Fi
Designer of the high street, WHY?
Did you not consider – even try
To provide a simple thing, like a Bus Lay By

Victims of Justice
(Printed Lennox Herald)

Victims suffer torment of the soul
While perpetrators get out on parole
Full sentences they never complete
Back on the street, more crimes to repeat

Rehabilitation, liberals cry
No regard for the murdered who die
And the families that remain
Suffering daily with loss and pain

Advocating prisoners, personal phones
Delivery of drugs to prison by drones
Shorter term sentences they spend
Soon back out, to re-offend

Victims of crime, all doing time
Though they don't go to jail
Justice and the courts fail
Criminals freed, out on bail

The Ring
(Printed Lennox Herald)

My origin began deep under the
earth
Miners mined and gave me birth
A shining metal from years untold
Yes, that is me, I am gold

Taken up out of the ground
The to a jeweller I was bound
By his trained and artful hand
I was fashioned into a wedding band

He then put me on public display
By placing me in a window on a tray
Under shining lights I did shine
Longing to hear someone say, Be
Mine

The that wonderful day did arrive
I felt accepted, I was alive
No longer in the window did I linger
O happy day when I was placed
upon a finger

This lady wore me with pride
For fifty seven years since she
became a bride
Although she's gone, there is no
gloom
It's been handed down as a family
heirloom

I remember I felt so grand
As my owner and husband walked
hand in hand
I felt the warmth of their love
I was glad I was hidden in a glove

Now my memories are getting dim
And I'm wearing a bit thin
Sadly the lady's hand I did grace
Has died, gone to a better place

I rejoice to see couples hand in
hands
At their wedding, exchanging gold
bands
I love to hear these words said
"With this ring, I the wed"

My loving couple did dance and sing
To others they did happiness bring
So it is them I am remembering
I am so happy, I was their ring

The Journey

From a mountain top high
I visualise with my mind's eye
I can cross borders and frontiers
Silently, peacefully, without fears

Travelling the world in my dreams
Sailing across oceans, fording
streams
In my memory store I find
Journeys I take, in my mind

Now I pause, darling, thinking of you
Our love together, honest and true
Remembering things we did and
said
The happiness of the life we led

You and I both flying high

Pathed by death when you did die
Your earthly journey did end
My darling, my lover, confidante and
friend

Serendipity

Was it by a happy accident?
Discovering you, was heaven sent
You my darling, beautiful inside out
In loving you I had no doubt

We met that night quite by chance
Your loveliness did me entrance
A wonderful beginning to our
romance
I took you home, glad I took the
chance

To be with you was pure pleasure
To me, you were beyond measure
You were my life's dream come true
I can never stop loving you

How I miss your smiling face

The warmth of your loving embrace
Lost with you in a passionate kiss
Darling with you, life was pure bliss.

<u>History Rewritten</u>
<u>(Printed Lennox Herald)</u>

Ross Greer, at 24 years of age
Attempts to rewrite our history and
heritage
He seeks to destroy Winston
Churchill
A man whose boots he could not fill

September 1939, war looking feeling
of fear
Thankfully this country was not led
by Ross Greer
This young Green MP attempts to
smear
Churchill a leader beyond compare

Boy Greer, unelected - List MP
Without Churchill's stand where
would you be?

Part of Hitler youth, the Nazi plan
You would be a slave speaking
German

Greer green MP with poor
credentials
Would swap his country for a bowl of
lentils
Who will history remember?
Winston Churchill, and honourable
member

Some names please note
Would have left you without a vote
Hitler Himmler Goebbels
Heidreich, Eichmann, Stalin.

Unexpected Moment

That unexpected moment, I entered
the room
I saw you, vision of loveliness, my
heart went boom
I offered to take you home, you said
yes

That magical moment in time I bless

We lingered at your gate, we kissed,
and it was fate
I fell in love with you, asked you for
a date
I was early, you were late
Your name was Marion, nicknamed
Kate

I am happy that night I took the
chance
We were bound together, locked in
romance
Our love blossomed like a flower in
full bloom
You became my bride, I was your
groom

For fifty seven years we stood the
test of time
Darling I am so thankful you were
mine
Dementia robbed you of memories
we had

I still remember that unexpected
moment, I'm so glad.

Grief Encounter
(Printed Lennox Herald)

We met briefly today
Having a coffee in a café
You were sitting in a mobility chair
You smiled, I wanted to share

Inner thoughts and feeling
From deep within my being
The loss of my darling wife of fifty
seven years
Finding it hard to hold back the tears

Then you shared your grief, I
remember
Your husband died, last September
I gave you a single red rose

In the midst of our sadness and grief
We shared in that moment so brief

Kindred spirits silently sharing our losses

Bringing my joy and relief when I give
Single red roses to ladies I meet
In cafes and in the street

<u>Spellbound</u>
<u>(Printed Lennox Herald)</u>

Excited, enthralled, entranced
Now you feel you've been romanced
You're on a road of mixed directions
Stirring your feelings and affections
This without doubt, a lovely lass
Way above your class
You have just asked her out
How did you dare?
How with her other beaus do you compare
She is a stoater and a stunner
Will I be a non-runner

Will I win her as my own?
Or end up being alone
I must take this chance
Seize the moment while I'm in a
trance

<u>Epitaph to Red Rose Man</u>
<u>(Printed Lennox Herald)</u>

Hello, I must tell you to my surprise
On Facebook, just heard of my
demise
I know that out there are trolls
Sorry to disappoint, -- Cancel
sausage rolls

For now the end is not near
I am still alive, I'm still here
It is not my final curtain
Not popped my clogs or gone for a
burton

It may just be a mistake
So you can cancel the wake
I might have missed the bus

But my middle name is NOT
Lazarus

When I go, whenever that will be
I hope you will remember me
May I suggest and propose
You will give someone a single red
rose

<u>Chance meeting</u>

I met a woman today
Stopped to have a chat
I gave her a single red rose
She said, I needed that

I explained the reason for the rose
In memory of someone who was
very close
With every rose I give with care
I hear a story they want to share

Some are happy, some are sad

They thank me for the rose and say
You have really made my day
I am so glad we have met this way

Exchange a smile and a hug
A kiss upon my cheek
My happiness is made complete
Today and all of this week

Brexititis

To everyone in the land
How much more can we stand
Incompetent governments can't
agree
So pass the buck to you and me

We had a vote, decided to leave
Politicians falter and deceive
Whatever they say we can't believe
Complete failure to achieve

What is happening, how do you feel
It is a nightmare, it is unreal
Second referendum, hard-soft
Brexit, no deal

My head is in a spin, my senses reel

EU treat us with contempt and
disdain
Their dealings with us are short and
abrupt
This organisation is utterly corrupt
Financial books never audited, will
end bankrupt

Daring to be different
(Printed Lennox Herald)

Can you make a difference?
Not just for the forty days of lent
Make right choices
Not sitting on the fence

When encountering darkness
Try to bring some light
Make every effort to bless
By doing what is right

When walking in the street
Bring joy to those you meet

Disperse sadness with a smile
Walk with a stranger, go the extra
mile

Jesus calls us to obey
Following Him day by day
Holy Spirit prompting guiding
Providing the words we should say

Lord when we meet people face to
face
Fill our conversation with grace
That they may see in us
The saving beauty of Jesus

Help us lord to make it known
That Jesus sits at your heavenly
throne
Salvation comes through Christ
alone
For our sins he did atone
He took the punishment we were
due
He died for me
He died for you

People

'People' who are we?
Simply put they are you and me
Single entities, married couples with
families
Merged together, forming societies

You and me, kith and kin
Beings born with shared origin
Baby girls and boys
White in prams, learn to throw out
their toys

Starting to crawl before they can
walk
Making funny noises before they can
talk
Inquisitive children, asking questions
a lot
Perplexed parents, all the answers
they have not

Tantrums from the terrible twos
Stamping feet, high pitched screams
Thought that was bad

Still to come, puberty, emerging
teens

People, now adults evolves
Affairs of the heart, now romantically
involved
Dating, walking out, holding hands
Engagement, marriage, exchanging
wedding gold bands

Travelling on, journey through life
Sharing love, man and wife
Children, one, two, three or four
Life's full circle – been here before

Years have come and gone
Aged couple – Darby and Joan
Alas one partner dies, passes on
The other is left all alone

Sharing Pain

I met a man deep in sorrow
His granddaughter died, no earthly
morrow
He expressed his pain and grief

Bereft, without present relief

This young girl of tender year
Died of cancer, loss of life, so young
Her life hardly begun
He finds this so hard to bear

A grandfather's worst nightmare
Yet he knows all is not doom and
gloom
This lovely lass passed into another
room
Into the realm of heaven above
Surrounded by God's gracious love

Facing this without hope or faith
Could he carry on, could he cope?
He cries out why this had to be
Lord – I'd rather you had taken me.

Internally Grateful

A picture taken of me internally
In the suite of endoscopy
I approached with fear and
trepidation

Until they sprayed my throat with
sedation

A friendly team of nurses
Claire, Dawn, Maggie, Jenny and
Lorna
Prepared me to receive the camera
Inserted with delicate precision
Procedure done without incision

Waiting time caused me fear and
doubt
Embarrassing moment taking my
dentures out
My head was north, my feet were
south
I felt a bit down in the mouth

I was thankful for the throat spray
coating
Not do much the air injection
Causing a bit of bloating
Thanks, nurses, sheer perfection

So thanks to the staff, one and all
At the Vale of Leven Hospital

Politicians hear me clear and loud
The local NHS did me proud

When it comes to making decisions
Politicians come to your senses
Public and hospitals come first
By cutting down your expenses

Happy Day
(Printed Lennox Herald)

Happy day, I'm on my way
To a radio interview with Kaye
Heart pumping adrenalin flowing
In a taxi to Radio Scotland I'm going

Like a tale from Jackanory
I am here to tell our love story
It's about the love of my life
Marion, my darling, my beautiful wife

What a joy to come and share
A story of our love so rare
Now all Scotland knows
Why I give out a red rose

In memory of Marion, my queen
In my heart you reign supreme
Sadly you died, now separated –
apart
Still residing deep within my heart

Equation of Love
(Printed Lennox Herald)

I know that one and one make two
But why am I attracted to you
Magnetism affects my heart
Drawn to you, never more to part

My emotions are all over the place
When I gaze upon your lovely face
Your inner beauty shone through
Can't stop falling in love with you

Your blonde hair, skin so fair
I feel I'm walking on air
Floating high on a cloud
Being with you I feel so proud

With you my love, I soared so high
Broke my heart, our final goodbye
You're still in my heart, I can dream
Thinking of you, my love supreme

Thankful for that night we met
Wonderful life, full of love, no regret
Thankful that wonderful chance
To share our love, in true romance

<u>The Fantasist</u>

When did you enter this fantasy
land?
When did your life get out of hand?
When did you enter this realm of
pretenses?
Was it because of unlawful driving
offences?

A person with educational ability
Yet unable to accept responsibility
Guilty of offences, you try to deny
Is this the reason you lie and lie?

Making friends, you turn on the charm
Are you unaware you cause them harm?
Telling the truth, are you incapable
In fact are you mentally unstable

When will all this deceit stop?
By the way, where is my laptop?
When from you the truth I will get
When will you return my tablet?

Will this saga have a happy ending?
Depends on when you stop pretending
So that my twilight years may end in peace
This mock friendship must cease
Farewell from me, my last goodbyes
My great escape from your deceit and lies

Sunshine and Showers

Seated by a window in the Rose and
Crown
Looking on the beer garden, sun is
blazing down
It is very hot behind the glass
Hold on a minute, what has come to
pass

Suddenly the sky darkens, now the
law of sods
Rain is falling, like proverbial stair
rods
Rain is bouncing from the tables
Like as scene from Aesops fables

This usual suntrap like a swimming
pool
No one will be sitting on a wet stool
Within minutes, sun shines again
The rain is out of sight, running
down a drain

The beer garden is deserted, a
lonely sight

Now the sun has got his hat on, so
bright
Gradually the warmth dries out the
sodden scene
It's as if the rain has never been

Bright sunshine now reigns supreme
Did this really happen or was it a
dream
Sometime things happen then
disappear
By the way, where did I leave my
beer?

Drinking time is over, time to go
home
What will be the ending of this silly
poem?
I know, I've just walked out of the
door
Would you believe it, into another
downpour?

<u>Shining love</u>

Let your love shine on me
Lift my darkness, let me see
Remove the gloom of dark night
Draw near my darling bright

Amidst the storms of life be near
By my side, please be here
Anchored safe, beside the shore
Content, together evermore

When dark clouds gather
And my spirit feels so low
I've lost my direction, where to go
Bring your love to me, let it show

Together we can start anew
I deeply love only you
Looking to our future, not the past
Together forever, our love will last

<u>Happy Birthday Hazel</u>

Hazel, happy birthday cheer
I believe you had one last year
Thankful for the time given
This year reaching seventy seven

May continue hale and hearty
Enjoy today your birthday party
Three score and ten the bible says
Enjoy your life of many days

Over this count as a plus
Each extra day is a bonus
The benefit of good health
Is much better than wealth

Today every moment savour
Birthday cake, enjoy the flavour
May bring your birthday to a close
Please accept my gift, a single red
rose

Springtime Song
(Printed Clydesider magazine)

Gazing from my window I can see
A glorious sight upon a tree
Apple blossom, blooming bright
Truly this is a wondrous sight

Reminding me, this is spring
When the birds begin to sing
Beyond the trees, green grassy hills
Covered in splendour with dancing
daffodils

Emerging from the wintertime cold
Bright clusters of crocus and
snowdrop unfold
Spring the season of anticipation
Filling hearts with hope and elation

Spring in motion – continuing
unchecked
Behold cherry blossom trees
bedecked
Adorned in glorious majestic pink

Season of rebirth and growth –
pause to think

Alas the beautiful blossoms did not
last
Blown away by March winds blast
Now upon the ground a carpet of
pink is cast
This scene, totally unsurpassed

May we continue to enjoy Nature's
power?
When tiny bud emerges as a flower
Nature untouched by human hand
Set in motion from the heavenly
realm
Surely creator God is at the helm

**<u>Four Seasons in
Remembrance of Me
(to Marion – just after her
death)</u>**

December it is wintertime
When you left me, the end of the line

Growth has ceased, a time of wrapping
Up against the cold. Bowls of soup, steak pie,
Christmas Pud, Christmas time,
The birth of Christ remembered
Friends, family,
In these things we remember Marion

Springtime the season of awakening
Vibrant new growth, trees budding
Spring flowers pushing through stubborn sod
The joy of new life, give thanks to God
In these things we remember Marion

Summertime, in the warmth of the sunny days
With the beautiful flowers on display
Children playing in the park
Sweet singing of the lark
Joy of life lived to the full
In these things we remember Marion

Autumn time, autumn leaves falling,
red and gold
Trees left bare and stark
Walk in the park, lights shining in the
dark.

Marion, remembered for your lovely
smile
Your beautiful face, your nature full
of grace
Your faith in God, your love of Jesus
Your loving care for children
Your life has been a wonderful story
May you now rest in heaven's glory?

<u>Dumbarton Town</u>

At the confluence of the rivers –
Leven and Clyde
Stands Dumbarton town
Shipbuilders of world renown
Craftsmen, built with pride

Surrounding area of manufacturing
excellence

Even employment by the Ministry of
Defence
The products were a wide variety
Bringing work and prosperity to
society

May I bring to your attention?
The list below is worth a mention
Places of employment of yesteryear
Sadly gone, no longer here.

Glass works, whisky distillery, beer
brewery
Shipbuilding, engines, boilers, boiler
tubes
Helicopters, aeroplanes, hovercraft
Cars, valves, soot blowers
Adding machines, clocks, lenses,
cameras, film
Potato crisps, lemonade, milk
dairies, leather bags
Prefab houses, coal gas, torpedoes,
whisky bottling
Yachts, marine craft, hosiery, silk
dye works

Forge, foundry, farming, and power generation
Many places of work, old and new.

Oh I nearly forgot – Unemployment Bureau

I'm Feeling Better, so I wrote a Letter
(Printed Lennox Herald)

May I once again express my complete and utter admiration for all the staff at Vale of Leven Hospital?

I'll start at the very beginning, do-ray-me
I was admitted in to A&E and Dr Ali Shah did see
After tests and examinations Dr Ali made his decision
To sanction my admission
I moved to ward three, or was it two?
I found myself in the AMRU

There I was beset with puzzlement
Trying to determine the sister's accent
She explained it was one of the Heinz 57 variety
A globe-trotting family all of their days
That's why she speaks in 57 different ways
Upward and onwards to Lomond Ward
The A-Team a well-trained troupe
Compliments to the chef for a good bowl of soup
Of every meal I can't complain
I'd gladly eat them all again
Well presented, of good taste
I cleared my plate, no waste.
I then became quite confused
As duplicate names were used
Staff nurse Katie – one and two
Don't ask what Katie did next, I haven't got a clue
There was Countess Dracula
A taker not giver of blood
Her favourite and main aims

Were to search for veins
Then there is Janice, a lady with
great flair
Who is very good at cutting hair?
With zest and zeal sets about her
task
Above and beyond the call of duty,
no matter what you asked
Question; Are we still engaged
Humour never far away
I saw curtains changed four times
one day
Orchestrated by the wee wummin
Alison
She is the controller of infection
Curtain changes are often daily
And when they are opened they
send for Jackie Baillie
Well within her remit and scope
Reported to have attended the
opening of an envelope
To bring this saga to an end
May I be your Union agent?
To campaign for NHS workers'
wages to be raised by 11 per cent
Because you are worth it.

Perverse Judgment

Hindsight is a marvellous thing
When the past we are remembering
It is so easy for us to say
Why did they do things that way?

We cannot judge in retrospect
We must take time to reflect
Our forerunners had hard decisions
to make
Many died in two world wars for our
sake.

Why do Uni students play the blame
game?
Seeking to deride, name and shame
Easy for you to talk the talk
Bygone heroes walked the walk

The statues you seek to destroy,
deface
In memory of people whose boots
you could not lace
Stop appraising them with modern
mindset

Don't say or do things you will regret.

Remember well, lest we forget.

Bungle in the Jungle

Following indefatigable George, the Cat
Kezia dons her celebrity hat
MSP, strutting her stuff
Should have appeared in Call My Bluff.

Shallow people, lacking pride
Taking the public for a ride
Treating the electorate with disrespect
Enjoy your diet of tasty raw insect

Perhaps you'll find your true vocation
Still being financed by the nation
People of Scotland, come to your senses

Will Keiza be claiming parliamentary
expenses?

Workers unite, keep on striving
While your MSP is in the jungle,
skiving
In this her latest claim to fame
Please, No – not in our name.

Knowing You

Knowing you and the love we
shared
Our closeness and how much you
cared
Together in a world of bliss
Totally embraced in a loving kiss

Filled with the feeling of belonging
Filling my heart with great longing
Lifted high to realms above
Locked together forever in love

That loving look from your beautiful
eyes
Brought me into a place of paradise

Two lovers completely entwined
Two as one, totally combined

Our love from beginning to end
Like a magic potion, a magical blend
You and I climbed mountains high
I miss you darling, thank you for our
long goodbye

If our parting be sad sweet sorrow
I lift up my eyes to see our eternal
morrow
My longing hope keeps me going
My memories of you, I'm knowing.

Like a summer Breeze

You came to me like a summer
breeze
With you I was completely as ease
A perfect match, hand in glove
Was the closeness of our love?

We kissed, sent my senses reeling
Overcome by a tingling feeling

In my dreams it is you I'm seeing
Totally enthralled, loving you with all
of my being

Two young lovers, filled with passion
You were so chic, the height of
fashion
I remember a dress, mohair, royal
blue
A picture, perfect, beautiful were you

You were utterly divine
Dream of my life, you were mine
I loved being with you all the time
Blending together, like poetry in
rhyme

Queen of Hearts

Darling you were queen of my heart
Broken when you died, now we are
apart
The emptiness I feel on my own
Now I am all on my own, alone.

Now I know loneliness in life
Since I lost my beloved wife.
You filled my life, you were supreme
My Darling, My heart's Queen

People say time will heal
But Darling, this I do not feel
Inside is still death's ache
I remember you, with every breath I
take

With you I tasted life so sweet
We were surely destined to meet
Our journey together was meant to
be
Finally to be reunited, you and me.

Once Upon a Time
(Printed Lennox Herald)

In a land of hope and glory
A country with a strong history
United together we did stand
Believing in a free and democratic
land

Long before the Unites States of
Europe
We traded with the world wide, we
did cope
Being dominated by the EU, down a
slippery slope
Let us nor resurrect a land of hope

The EU, a collective of corruption
Hell bent on the UK's destruction
Germany tried this before by armed
force
Now with economic sanctions
coerce

Let us stand together once more
Recognise the enemy at the door
The EU fears a domino effect
When we leave, others will also defect.

<u>The Look</u>

The look that says I love you
The look that says you care
The feeling of two hearts in time
The feeling of true love, so rare

That glowing feeling deep inside
Knowing you love me, fills me with pride
My feelings for you I cannot hide
Darling, Please, be my lovely bride

Let's enjoy this life together
In love, now and forever
Draw close, hold my hand
Darling I want to be your husband

Let's hold on to our romantic bliss

Let's draw close in the warmth of a
kiss
My darling, my love, you I adore
Till the end of time, for now,
evermore.

<u>My Hero</u>

Lord I once kept you
In the shadows
I was content to go
My way
I kept all your love
At bay.

I was the one who
Sought glory
You're the one that took
My pain
You were without a face
Or name

But know I know that you're
My hero
You're all I need

In life
Now I can fly higher than
An eagle
You are the wind beneath
My wings

I was the one with all the
Hang Ups
Never seeing things
Quite clear
Out of control and living life
In fear

But then you showed me
All your glory
You reached out and
Touched my heart
I was blind but now
I See

Now I know that you're
My hero
You are all I need
In Life
I can fly higher than
An eagle

You are the wind beneath
My wings

Our Secret Places

We wandered together in the park
The brilliance of the moon outshone
the dark
To us it was a secret sacred place
We drew together, shared a warm
embrace

How lovely, your beautiful face
My memory returns to this haunting
place
In my loneliness and solitude
I remember our love, it was so good.

Our first meeting was quite by
chance
Blossoming in to a sweet romance
Remembering our first kiss
Completed by our wedded bliss

Together fifty seven loving years
Sharing love and joy, a few tears

Then that fateful day you died
I said goodbye to my beautiful bride.

Farewell my love, it seems so final
But I know our love is eternal.

<u>Children are beautiful people</u>

Watching children, tiny tots
Learning to walk and talk
Emerging like a butterfly from a
cocoon
Their innocent smiles light up a
room.

Each individual girl and boy
Bring us so much love and joy
Free spirits unfettered by convention
Having a natural ability to get
attention

Through their childhood may we
nurture?
The children are the future
Teach them to love and care

Kind to others, and to share

As adults we think we know it all
Remember pride comes before a fall
Learn to be more like a child
Gentle, loving, meek and mild.

Mistress in Distress (Printed Lennox Herald)

What a tangled web we weave
When we practice to deceive
Thinking you are the only one
When this affair has begun

Feelings of great exhilaration
Heart fluttering filled with elation
No thought for the marriage you will
break
As another woman's man you will
take

Enjoying the bliss from his attention

Conveniently forgetting the wife he
omits to mention
Doubts creep in, is this love or just
lust
Is this a man you can trust?

What about the days you are left
alone
You cannot call him on the phone
Mistresses of the world beware
So often you end up in despair

What lies ahead, trouble and strife?
He has no intention of leaving his
wife
How many Christmas days spent on
your own?
Ending once again all alone

Time goes by, months then years
Your dream of love, your heart now
broken
Bereft of love, lonely and forsaken
Alas all ends in tears

He tells you that you are the love of
his life
Yet still goes on holiday with his wife
In this relationship what can be
believed
Will end in sadness, totally deceived

Acknowledgements

- To Lisa, for putting all these together
- To the Lennox Herald for the support over the years in printing my poems in the local paper
- To everyone who bought Love for Life. I really appreciate it.

Printed in Great Britain
by Amazon

18743951R00071